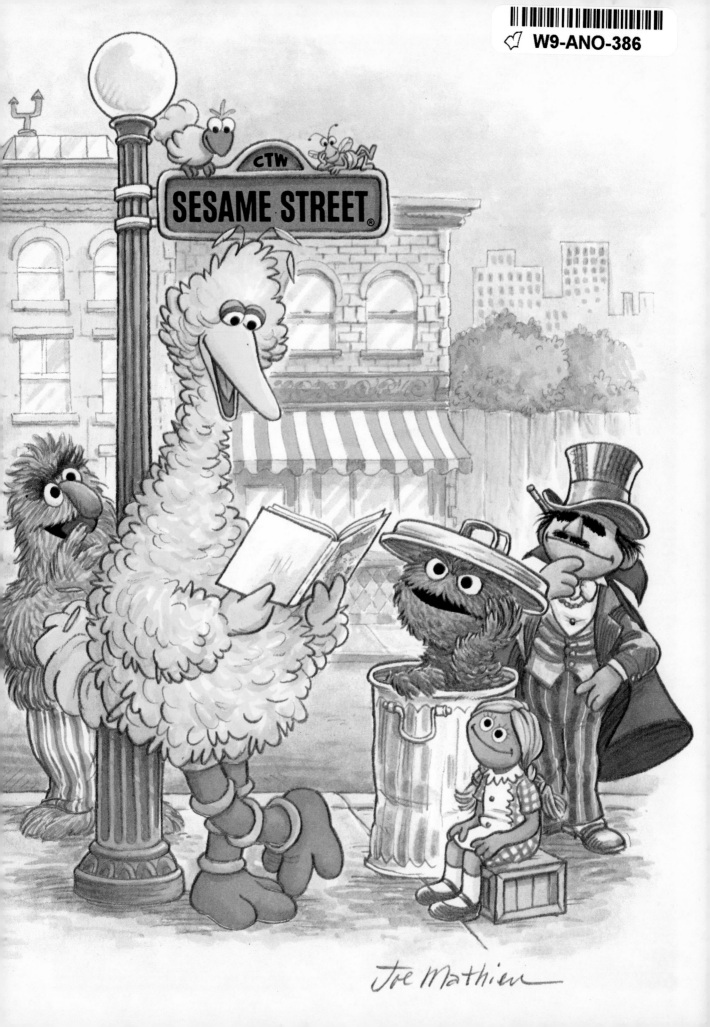

THE SESAME STREET® LIBRARY

With Jim Henson's Muppets

VOLUME 9

FEATURING
THE LETTER S
AND THE NUMBER
9

Children's Television Workshop/Funk & Wagnalls, Inc.

WRITTEN BY:
Michael Frith
Jerry Juhl
Emily Perl Kingsley
Sharon Lerner
Nina B. Link
Albert G. Miller
Jeffrey Moss
Norman Stiles
Jon Stone
Daniel Wilcox

ILLUSTRATED BY:
Mel Crawford
A. Delaney
Mary Lou Dettmer
Michael Frith
David Gantz
Tim and Greg Hildebrandt
Joseph Mathieu
Harry McNaught
Michael J. Smollin
Caroll Spinney

PHOTOGRAPHS BY:
Charles P. Rowan

 Published in the United States by Random House, Inc., New York, and simultaneously in Canada by Random House of Canada Limited, Toronto, in conjunction with the Children's Television Workshop. Distributed by Funk & Wagnalls, Inc., New York, N.Y. Manufactured in the United States of America.

0-8343-0017-6

1 2 3 4 5 6 7 8 9 0

The Sock-maker and the Snuffle-upagus

Ss

*O*nce there was a poor, tired old Sock-maker. One day, he promised to sew socks for the whole town, but by evening he was just too tired to finish.

Oh, dear. I can't sew another sock. I hate to disappoint everybody, but I have to go to sleep. Goodnight, Big Bird.

Gee, poor Mr. Sock-maker.

Suddenly, there was a strange sound, a puff of smoke, and a flash of light, and there before Big Bird stood the Snuffle-upagus fairy.

Who are you?

I am the Snuffle-upagus fairy. I watch over poor, tired sock-makers everywhere.

The Snuffle-upagus fairy got right to work.

I'll sew those socks for him.

Look out! Your tail knocked those boxes over!

He sewed all night long.

And by sunup he had sewn every single sock.

And with the same puff of smoke and flash of light, the Snuffle-upagus fairy vanished as quickly as he had appeared.

Gee, do you have to vanish now? Mr. Sock-maker has never seen you, and I'm sure he'd like to meet you.

Sorry, Bird. We Snuffle-upagus fairies never stay to receive thanks.

When the Sock-maker woke up, was he ever surprised!

Why . . . who sewed my socks for me? And, by the way, who destroyed my store?

I can explain. . . . You see, during the night, the Snuffle-upagus fairy came, and he finished the socks, but he accidentally broke everything, and—

Oh, not that same Snuffle-upagus story again, Big Bird. There's no such thing as a Snuffle-upagus. You have some imagination!

And even though the Sock-maker didn't believe Big Bird, they all lived happily ever after . . . as soon as they had finished cleaning up the store.

Oscar's Bad-Time Junk Band

INTRODUCING...
LITTLE JERRY
AND THE
MONOTONES

Hey! I can't find my guitar—I feel MAD!

I can't find my drums—I feel SAD!

I can't find my maracas—I feel so BAD!

I think I left 'em on the bus—BOY, do I feel EMBARRASSED!

Oh, WOE!

WOE!

WOE!

WOE!

Listen! If you guys will promise to STOP THAT RACKET, I'll show you how to make some NEW instruments out of stuff from my famous trash collection.

Here's what you need to make a *guitar*:

A shoe box.

A cardboard tube from a roll of paper towels.

Large rubber bands (3 or 4).

A pencil.

Scissors.

Strong tape.

Here's how to make it

1. Cut a big hole in the middle of the lid of the box.

2. Stretch the rubber bands around the box, like this.

3. Put a pencil under the rubber bands...like this.

4. Tape the tube to one end of the box, like this.

   Your *Grouch Guitar* is ready to strum.

Here's what you need to make a *drum*:

An empty oatmeal box, or a coffee can with a plastic lid.

A longish loop of string.

Strong tape.

Paper and crayons.

Spoons or pencils.

Here's how to make it

1. Lay your long loop of string over the open top of the box, like this.
2. Tape the box top on tight, over the string.
3. Cut paper to fit around the box.
4. Decorate the paper with crayons.
5. Tape the paper around the box.

   Now put on your drum— and BEAT IT! (heh, heh)

Here's what you need to make *maracas*:

2 plastic spoons.

2 small containers with tops (you can use yogurt or sour cream cartons or small margarine or butter tubs).

Dried beans, small stones, macaroni— anything that will rattle.

Glue or tape.

Paper and crayons.

Here's how to make it

1. Cover the containers with decorated paper.

2. Glue or tape the paper in place.

   Punch a small hole in the bottom of each container.

3. Push the spoon handle through the hole, like this.

4. Put a handful of beans (or whatever) in the container.

5. Tape the tops on tight.

THE BOY, THE GIRL AND THE JELLYBEANS

CHAPTER TWO

One afternoon a boy was walking down the street. Just that morning he had given away his only bag of jellybeans, and that had made him feel very sad. But now he was beginning to get over it.

"Well, I don't have any jellybeans," he said to himself, "but that's okay. I can do without jellybeans. I'm a cool customer who doesn't need any jellybeans to get along in this world. I'm cool and I'm confident, brother, and nothing, NOTHING, can bother me."

He turned a corner and there he saw a girl. It was the very same girl he had given his bag of jellybeans to. And she still had it. She was clutching the bag in her hands and shaking like a thistle in a windstorm.

"Hey, girl," said the boy, "what's the matter with you?"

"I'm afraid!" said the girl. "I'm really, really scared. I'm so frightened that I've got goose bumps on my goose bumps."

"Huh!" said the boy. "I'm never afraid. I'm cool and I'm confident and nothing, NOTHING, bothers me. What's your problem?"

"*Problem?*" The girl's eyes grew wide. "A MONSTER is my problem. A great BIG monster has been after me."

"Pish-tosh," said the boy, "that's nothing to be afraid of. It certainly wouldn't frighten *me*."

"Oh yeah?" said the girl. "Did you ever have a monster after *you?*"

"Well . . . no," said the boy.

"There!" said the girl, still trembling with fear. "Then you don't know how scary it is. It's really frightening to have a great big UGLY monster after you."

"Phoo," said the boy. "I wouldn't be afraid. If he shows up again, I'll frighten *him* away."

"Really?" said the girl. "That's very nice of you. That's so nice, I'm going to give you back your jellybeans. Here, take them." She handed him the jellybeans and stopped trembling right away.

"I feel better now," she said. "I feel confident. I don't have a worry in the world."

"That's right," said the boy, "because there's nothing to worry about. Just be like me—I'm *never* afraid. *Yikes!*"

The boy screamed, for just then a great big ugly HAIRY monster came around the corner and headed straight for him.

"Oh me," moaned the boy. "Oh my, oh my. I'm so frightened. I'm so afraid that I'm afraid . . . I mean, I'm so scared that I'm scared . . . I mean, I'm so afraid that I'm trembling. Ohhhh."

"Really?" said the girl. "Well, I'm not at all afraid. Not a bit. Do you want to know why?"

"Why?" asked the shaking boy.

"Because," the girl answered, "that monster loves jellybeans. He was only after me because I had the jellybeans. But now *you* have the jellybeans. So he is not after ME any more. He is after

YOU. So you see, now I don't have anything to be afraid of." And, waving good-by, she skipped off down the street.

"JELLYBEANS!" roared the great big ugly hairy blue monster. "ME SMELL JELLYBEANS!"

"H-here, pal," squeaked the boy. "Have mine." And he quickly poured them all into the monster's great big ugly hairy blue paw.

"YUM! YUM!" roared the monster, swallowing them all in a gulp. "DELICIOUS! THANK YOU!" And he gave the boy a big wet hairy blue kiss right on the top of the head.

Then, arm in arm, the boy and the monster walked off down the street like a couple of old friends. And the boy wasn't frightened any more.

TO BE CONTINUED IN VOLUME 10.

Oscar's Shape Collection

Everybody thinks trash is no good for anything, but here are some pictures of ME showing some really GREAT STUFF from my famous TRASH collection! First—look at me holding that handsome old picture.

Somebody threw it out . . . and it's a perfectly good SQUARE!

There's a soggy comic book. It may not be much good for reading, but it's a great RECTANGLE.

And look at that rusty bicycle wheel. It's really a fine CIRCLE.

I had a hard time finding a TRIANGLE, but then somebody threw out this beautiful piece of old, smelly cheese. Isn't it great? I just don't understand why anybody would throw all this terrific stuff away.

The Brave Little Tailor

One day a little tailor was busily trying to sew. But seven flies kept buzzing around his head. So he grabbed his fly swatter and swatted the flies—killing all seven in one blow!

Feeling very proud of himself, the tailor made a patch that said "7," and stitched it to his coat. When he went out for a walk, everyone stared at the 7. "I killed seven in one blow!" explained the tailor proudly.

The people could hardly believe their ears. They told their king about the brave tailor. "We must ask him to kill those terrible giants on the hill," they said.

The king ordered the tailor to go and kill the two giants. "If you succeed," he said, "you can marry my daughter."

The tailor was frightened, but he *did* want to marry the king's daughter. So he went to look for the giants.

The tailor found the two giants under a tree —fast asleep and snoring. He climbed the tree and threw stones down at them.

"You monster!" roared the first giant at the second giant. "Why did you hit me?"

"*You* hit *me!*" cried the second giant. And he punched the first giant in the nose. The two giants began to fight. They fought until they both fell down with a crash.

The brave little tailor returned to the king and told him that the giants were dead.

"Then you and my daughter shall be married," said the king. And indeed they were.

SHAPES OF THINGS TO EAT

Listen, children, while I sing about
How I'm gonna eat
Three different **SHAPES** of things for lunch,
Here on Sesame Street.

Gonna start right in with a birdseed sandwich
Made on tasty rye . . .
Then top it off with a birdseed cookie
And a piece of birdseed pie!

Shape of the sandwich
Is a **SQUARE** . . .

Cookie
Is a **CIRCLE** neat . . .

Piece of pie
Is a **TRIANGLE** . . .
What a shapely treat!

Three different shapes
Of things to eat . . .

Here . . . on . . .

Sesame Street.

Cookie Monster's

Cookie Faces

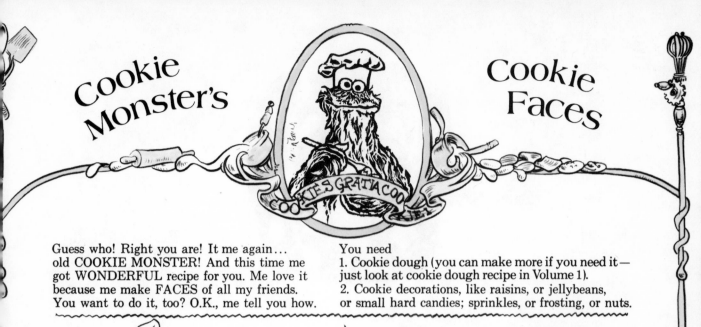

Guess who! Right you are! It me again...
old COOKIE MONSTER! And this time me
got WONDERFUL recipe for you. Me love it
because me make FACES of all my friends.
You want to do it, too? O.K., me tell you how.

You need
1. Cookie dough (you can make more if you need it—
just look at cookie dough recipe in Volume 1).
2. Cookie decorations, like raisins, or jellybeans,
or small hard candies; sprinkles, or frosting, or nuts.

Sprinkle flour on cloth and roll out your
dough on it (about ¼ inch thick).

Now cut out face shapes and peel away
extra dough, like this...

Now decorate them.   Raisins make good hair and eyes. Jellybean make
VERY tasty nose. Here are some of
my COOKIE FRIENDS...

ERNIE
Red
jellybean
nose.

BERT
Orange
jellybean
nose.

GROVER
Pink
jellybean nose.
And sprinkles
make him look
fuzzy.

SUSAN and GORDON
Peanuts make good noses
for people.

Now heat oven to 400 degrees,
put in cookies, and wait six to
eight minutes. Oh, boy! Me can
hardly wait to have my friends
for dinner!

Frith

The Story of the Nine Dragons

Once upon a time, in the faraway kingdom of St. George, there lived a baseball team. There were **9** players on the team.

TO THE PRACTICE FIELD

One day, as they reached their practice field, **9** dragons leaped out of the woods, breathing fire and smoke and yelling, *"Arkle-Snarkle Higgeldy Snoo!"*

This frightened the baseball players and they ran away. After all, you'd be frightened, too, if **9** dragons leaped out of the woods while you were playing baseball.

Every day when the **9** baseball players got to the ball field the same thing would happen.

After this had gone on for several weeks, one of the players decided it was time to do something about the dragons.

"I've got an idea how to get rid of those dragons," he said. And he told his idea to the other players.

So the next day, each of the **9** players got a big feather and went out to the baseball field.

When the **9** dragons jumped out of the forest, the **9** players took the **9** feathers and tickled the **9** dragons on their tummies. The dragons rolled over on their backs and giggled dragon-giggles and kicked their feet in the air.

But when they were finished being tickled, the dragons jumped up and breathed fire and smoke and yelled, *"Arkel-Snarkle Higgeldy Snoo,"* and frightened the players away again.

So the **9** baseball players decided that tickling the dragons wasn't such a good idea after all.

Suddenly, the team's right fielder (who also happened to be a dragon expert) stepped forward.

"I just happen to be a dragon expert," she said, "and I have an idea. Here's my dragon book. Why don't we look in it and see what *Arkle-Snarkle Higgeldy Snoo* means?"

"It's so crazy it just might work," said the third baseman.

The next day, when the **9** baseball players went out to the field, they pulled behind them a great big wagon with a cover over it.

Once again the **9** dragons jumped out of the woods, breathed fire and smoke, and yelled, *"Arkle-Snarkle Higgeldy Snoo! Arkle-Snarkle Higgeldy Snoo!!"*

The players quickly pulled the cover off the wagon and, lo and behold, there were **9** great big dragon-sized baseball caps, **9** great big dragon-sized baseball mitts, and **9** great big dragon-sized baseball bats!

For the right fielder's dragon book had told them that *"Arkle-Snarkle Higgeldy Snoo"* is dragon-talk for, "We want to play baseball, too!"

So every day the **9** baseball players went out to the baseball field and met the **9** dragons on the dragon team…and they played baseball.

So if you happen to be walking through the woods one day and **9** dragons jump out at you, breathing fire and smoke and yelling, "*Arkle-Snarkle Higgeldy Snoo,*" don't be afraid. Chances are they just want to play baseball!

The Grouch Garbage MOBILE

Roosevelt Franklin, Doctor

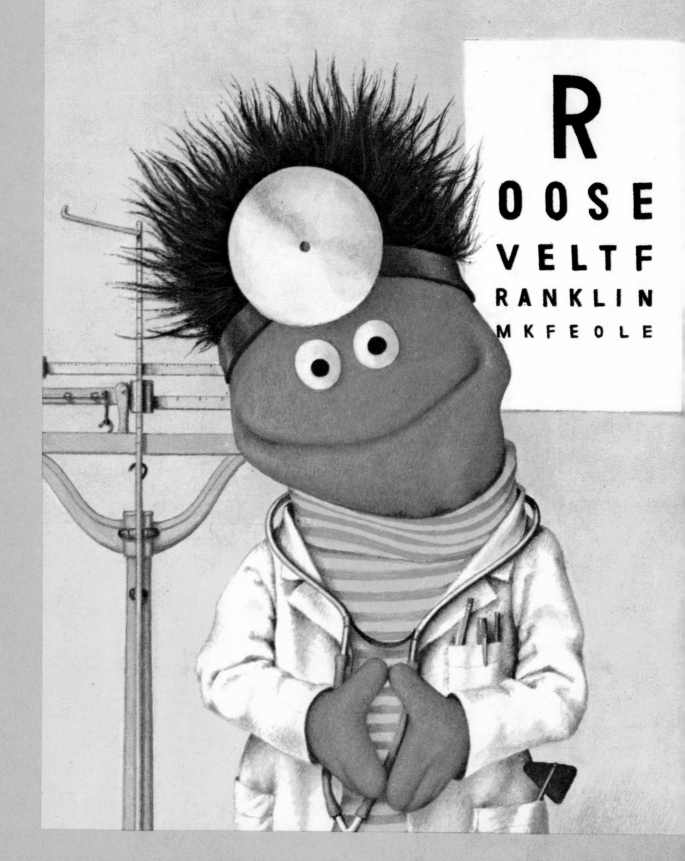

Sherlock Hemlock
in
The Case of the Lost Lunch

Boo-hoo!

E-Gad! A bird in distress! What is the matter, Little Bird?

Oh, Mr. Sherlock Hemlock, sir, my friend Big Bird invited me to his nest for a delicious birdseed lunch, and I don't know how to get there. And I'm getting VERY hungry.

Never fear, Little Bird. I, Sherlock Hemlock, the World's Greatest Detective, will help you find the way to Big Bird's nest.

Oh, look! There's a trail of birdseed on the ground. Maybe Big Bird dropped it on the way home from Mr. Hooper's store.

E-Gad!
A trail of birdseed!
Perhaps Big Bird dropped it on his way home from Mr. Hooper's store. If we follow it, we may find our way to Big Bird's nest.

Look! Mr. Hemlock...
(munch, munch)

MUNCH! MUNCH!

The birdseed leads...

(gobble, gobble)
UNDER this fence.

(smack, gulp)
Look—OVER the bridge...

(crunch, yum)
He must have gone DOWN this hill...

(munch, crunch)
and UP these stairs...

(yum, yum) and IN this door...

(yum, yum)
and OUT that door...
and there he is!

HELP LITTLE BIRD FIND HIS WAY TO BIG BIRD'S NEST

Hey, everybody, come here. I've got something to show you!

Oscar's Bowling Contest

I just won the Annual Grouch Bowling Contest. Let me show you my amazing style!

Luis, you set up those milk cartons on the sidewalk.

Susan, hand me that big wad of tin foil. Now— watch this!

Oh, Oscar! Your...uh... beautiful trophy is broken!

Hey, will you look at that? That's terrific! Why didn't I think of that before?

What you need:

6 empty milk cartons

A ball of tin foil

Paper and pencil for keeping score

How to play:

1. Set up cartons like this...
2. Stand about ten steps away from the cartons.
3. Each player takes a turn trying to knock down the cartons with the tin foil ball.
4. Count how many cartons you've knocked down and write it on the scorecard.
5. After each turn, set up the cartons for the next player.
6. The player who has knocked down the most cartons after three turns WINS!

Luis's Fingerprint Pictures

Hola, Big Bird. I have a great idea. Let's make fingerprint pictures.

Oh! That sounds like fun. How do you do that, Luis?

Well, first we have to make some fingerprint paint.

We need

½ cup of flour

¼ cup of water

Mix them up and add

½ cup of liquid detergent or liquid laundry starch.

Then add food coloring or poster paint

and mix it *all* up together.

Now get some paper, and you're ready to make fingerprint pictures.

When they dry, you can draw faces on them.

But, Luis . . .

Just a minute, Big Bird. You can make fingerprint designs, or . . .

But, Luis . . .

Well, what is it Big Bird?

I don't have fingers, like you! I'm a bird, and . . .

WAIT! I bet I could make FOOT prints though. Let me see . . .

¡Oh, qué desorden!

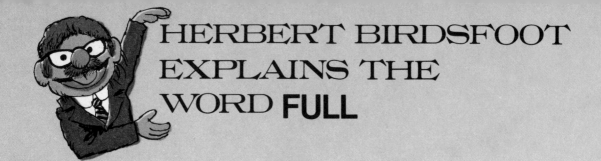

HERBERT BIRDSFOOT EXPLAINS THE WORD **FULL**

Hi, there. This is your friend, Herbert Birdsfoot. I'm here to tell you about the word **FULL**.

As you can see, this glass is **FULL**. It's **FULL** of yummy strawberry.

Strawberry soda?

Hey, *don't.*